KU-442-766

· CREATIVE CRAFTS ·

FUN WITH
NATURE

· HEATHER AMERY ·

HAMLYN

HANDY HINTS

This book gives you lots of wonderful ideas about how to make all sorts of nature projects. You can make them exactly as they are in the book, or you can use the ideas to create your own unique versions.

You will need to use sharp knives, scissors, varnish and boiling water to make some of the projects in this book. Be careful when you use these things and always make sure that an adult is there to help you.

ACKNOWLEDGEMENTS

Projects made by Jan Bridge, Gail Rose, Brian Robertson and Julia Worth
Photographs by Peter Millard
Illustrations by Joanna Venus

HAMLYN CHILDREN'S BOOKS
Editor : Jane Wilsher
Designer : Julia Worth
Production Controller : Mark Leonard

Published in 1994 by
Hamlyn Children's Books
an imprint of Reed Children's Books,
Michelin House, 81 Fulham Road, London SW3 6RB
and Auckland, Melbourne, Singapore and Toronto

Copyright © 1994 Reed International Books Ltd.

All rights reserved. No part of this publication may be reproduced, stored in a retrieval system, or transmitted, in any form or by any means electronic, mechanical, photocopying, recording, or otherwise, without the prior permission of the copyright holders.

Hardback ISBN 0 600 58494 1
Paperback ISBN 0 600 58495 X

Printed in Italy by LEGO

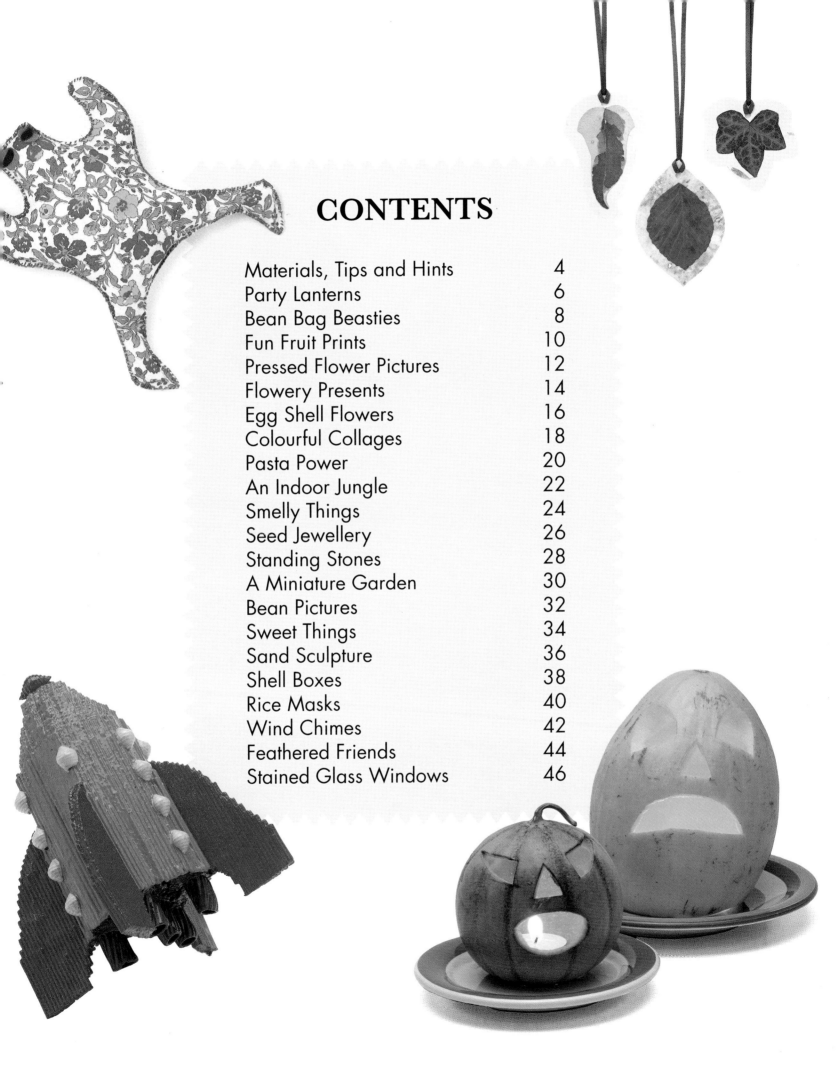

CONTENTS

MATERIALS, TIPS AND HINTS

This book shows you how to make all sorts of interesting things with leaves, flowers, seeds, shells and even sand. It's full of ideas for making presents and unusual decorations, and for growing your own indoor gardens and jungles.

Look out for things to collect when you are in the country, a park in the middle of a busy city, or a garden, or by the sea or a lake. Look for feathers, ferns, grasses, nuts, pine cones, reeds, corn stalks, small stones and pebbles.

Before you pick flowers or leaves in a garden, always ask first. Just take a few of each sort. Remember, it is against the law to pick some wild flowers, even ones you think are weeds. If you are not sure, ask an adult. Look at indoor plants, too. Many of them have lovely leaves.

Be patient when you are growing things. It always take a few days or more before you can see any growth. Put them in a warm place with lots of light but not in direct sunlight.

Glue

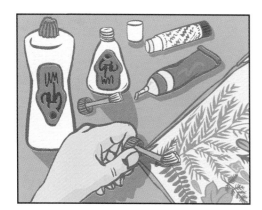

Use children's clear glue for making most things. PVA glue is good for sticking and for painting things to give them a hard, shiny finish. You can buy PVA in most art and craft shops.

Paint

Poster paint comes in dry blocks or ready-mixed in pots. It is cheap, covers well, dries quickly and washes off with water. You can buy it in most stationer's shops, and in art, craft or toy shops.

Scissors

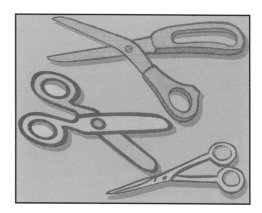

You will need scissors for cutting flower and leaf stems, paper and cardboard. You will need sharp pointed scissors for poking holes in cardboard, and small ones for cutting fiddly things.

Non-shiny sticky tape hardly shows when you stick it down.

Look out for feathers with beautiful patterns.

HANDY HINTS

Cut flowers and leaves with garden scissors or secateurs. If you try to break them off, you may damage the plants.

Cut flowers and leaves with long stems. You can shorten them later when you are making a decoration.

Ask first before you use the kitchen to make the sugar and chocolate-coated fruits. Remember to wash and tidy up after you have finished.

Knives

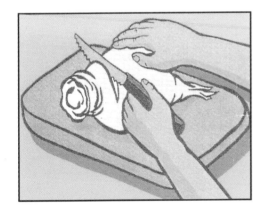

You will need a kitchen knife for cutting vegetables. Always cut downwards with the knife pointed away from you on to a chopping board. If something is difficult to cut, ask an adult to help you.

Collection box

Keep the dry things you collect together safe in a box. This will help to stop them from getting broken. They will also be in one place and ready to use when you want to make something.

Getting ready

Painting and gluing is a messy business. Spread plenty of old newspapers over the table or floor where you are working. Also, wear an old T-shirt or an apron to protect your clothes.

PARTY LANTERNS

Often Hallowe'en is a day for a party when people dress up as witches and wear tall hats and black cloaks. A fun Hallowe'en party decoration is a lantern carved out of a melon with a scary, grinning face. For a really dramatic effect, make lots of different types and sizes of lantern heads, then turn off the lights and watch their scary faces glow in the dark.

Things you need

A melon, either a water-melon, honeydew or ogen melon
A knife
A bowl
A large metal spoon or ice-cream scoop
A felt-tip pen
A night light with a metal base
A box of matches
An old saucer, not a plastic one

Make your lanterns look happy, scary or frightening.

HANDY HINTS

Before the party begins, ask an adult to light the night light. Put the lantern in a safe place where it won't be knocked over and remember to blow out the night light when you've finished with it.

A small melon lantern

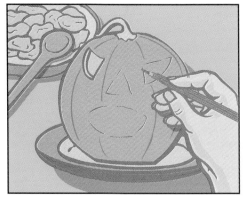

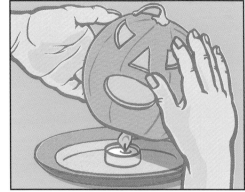

1. Ask an adult to help you cut away a small round shape in the bottom of the melon which is big enough to fit the night light. Scoop out the seeds .

2. Scoop out the flesh until the melon is hollow. Keep the flesh to eat later. Draw a big mouth, nose and eyes on the melon. Ask an adult to cut out the shapes.

3. Put the night light on a plate. Ask an adult to light it and carefully place the lantern on top. Put your lantern in a safe place away from draughts.

Water-melon lantern

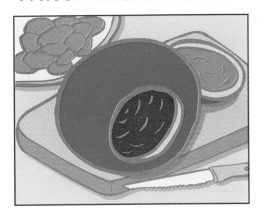

1. Ask an adult to help you cut the top off the melon. Scoop out the flesh from inside the melon and save it to eat later.

2. Turn the melon upside down so it rests on its base. Draw shapes on it. Carefully cut out the shapes a little at a time.

3. Cut a hole in the base of the melon for the night light and push it in. Ask an adult to light it and put the top back on the melon.

Use different kinds of melons with different-coloured skins.

A star and moon water-melon lantern

BEAN BAG BEASTIES

You can make all sorts of fat, squashy animals from fabric shapes filled with dried beans, peas or rice. Try mixing and matching your fabrics and thinking about how the fabric feels. You could try making a sleek cat bean bag, ready to be stroked, from a smooth velvety fabric.

Things you need

Pieces of different fabric, some patterned, some plain
Ric-rac braid and scraps of felt
Thin paper to make the pattern
Scissors and pins
A needle and thread
Rice or dried beans

Glue on felt eyes and ric-rac scales

A fat fish full of beans

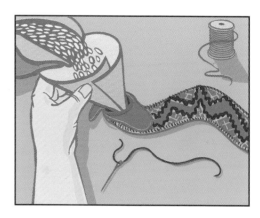

Slithery snake

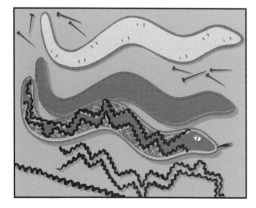
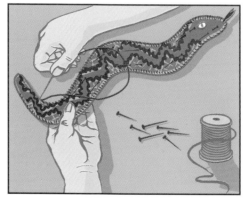

1. Draw and cut out the shape of a fat, slithery snake on paper. Pin the paper to the fabric and cut out two pieces. Glue scraps of fabric and ric-rac on the top piece.

2. Pin the pieces together. Sew the two sides of the snake together with close small stitches, all around the edges of the fabric. Leave a 4cm opening at one end.

3. Use a small piece of paper to make a funnel. Slip it inside the opening and pour in enough rice to fill the snake. Sew up the opening with small close stitches.

Fat fish

  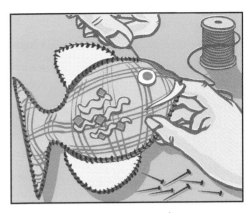

1. Draw and cut out a fish shape and a fin shape on paper. Pin the fish shape to one fabric and the fin shape to another. Cut out two fish shapes and two fin shapes.

2. Decorate the top fish shape with ric-rac and felt. Pin the pieces together. Sew around the edge of the fish with close small stitches. Leave a 4cm opening at one end.

3. Sew around the outside edge of each fin, then sew them to the fish. Pour the rice through a paper funnel into the opening. Sew up the opening with close stitches.

This leaping frog can also sit up on his bean bag bottom!

Glue a long felt tongue on to your snake.

HANDY HINTS

It's best to use fabric which does not fray.

Fill your bean bags with small beans such as aduki beans rather than large butter beans, which will be too lumpy.

Try to make your stitches as small and close as possible, otherwise the rice or beans may fall out. Use a brightly coloured thread which goes well with the fabric.

Round bean bag ladybirds

FUN FRUIT PRINTS

You can make your own pretty wrapping paper, headed notepaper, cards and labels by printing lots of patterns with fruit. Try using hard fruits, such as apples and pears, or experiment with peppers and mushrooms. Think about the patterns different fruits and vegetables will make when they are cut in half.

Things you need

A lemon, plum and other small firm fruit
A sharp knife
Kitchen paper
Poster paints
An old saucer
Scrap paper
A folder to print on
Plain notepaper
Plain envelopes
Sheets of plain paper
Cotton ribbon

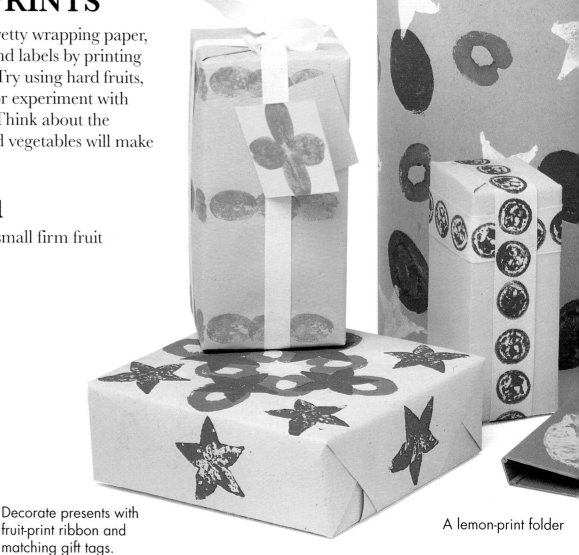

Decorate presents with fruit-print ribbon and matching gift tags.

A lemon-print folder

Fruity folder

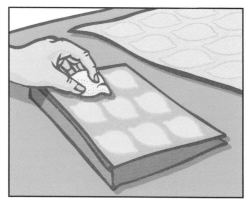

1. To make a printing pad, fold up a sheet of kitchen paper and put it on a plate. Pour thick paint on to the paper so that it is completely covered.

2. Cut a lemon in half from end to end. Take out the pips. Blot any juice on to kitchen paper. Press the cut side of the lemon on to the pad to cover it with paint.

3. Press the cut side down on to a sheet of scrap paper to practise printing. Then make prints on the folder, pressing the lemon on to the pad when it needs more paint.

Wrapping paper made with different fruit prints.

Cover a gift box with fruity paper and tie a ribbon into a big bow.

Star fruit stationery

HANDY HINTS

Try cutting the fruit in different ways. You can cut it from end to end or across to make different patterns.

Use paint that is thick and sticky and not too runny.

If the fruit is juicy when you cut it, dry the cut side with kitchen paper.

You will make better, more even prints if you put a wad of newspaper under the paper you are printing on.

When cutting fruit in half, try making the cut as straight as you can so that the surface is flat and prints cleanly.

Fruity paper

Print a star fruit pattern down the sides of sheets of notepaper. Then use the same fruit-cut to make matching prints on the front of some envelopes.

To make wrapping paper, cut one type of fruit in half and print a pattern on the paper. Then print more shapes with a different fruit and different-coloured paint.

You can use fruit-printed paper to wrap up all sorts of presents. Try using small fruit to print along coloured ribbon. This works best on cotton-based ribbon.

PRESSED FLOWER PICTURES

Pick small colourful flowers and different sorts of green leaves, grasses, ferns and bracken to press and make into pictures. Try using flowers of only one or two colours, or make a picture from many different-coloured flowers that go well together.

Things you need

Flowers and leaves
Sheets of clean blotting paper or old newspapers
Heavy books, thick paper or thin card
Glue, scissors, cling film

HANDY HINTS

Choose flowers which don't have thick, juicy heads. If you want to press big flowers such as roses, carefully pull off the petals and press them separately.

Always pick flowers and leaves when they are quite dry. Look for autumnal leaves, too.

A summer meadow picture

Pressing flowers

1. Lay the flowers and leaves on the blotting paper or newspaper. Let the stems curve naturally, but don't let the petals overlap.

2. Put another sheet of blotting paper or newspaper gently on top of the flowers and leaves. Make sure you do not disturb them.

3. Put some large heavy books on top of the sheets. Leave the flowers to press for at least two weeks before you use them.

Making pictures

1. Cut the paper or card to the size you want the picture to be. Lay the flowers and leaves on it. Move them about until you like the arrangement.

2. Dab a little glue on the backs of the flowers and the leaves, and down the stems. Carefully press them down in place on the paper or card.

3. Gradually build up the layers of flowers, carefully sticking them down as you go. This picture is made from rose petals, with green leaves poking from behind.

Glue your flowers and leaves on to coloured paper or card.

FLOWERY PRESENTS

When you have pressed some flowers, you can use them to decorate lots of different presents, such as cards, notepaper and book covers. Make a matching set of stationery and give it away as a special present.

Things you need

Pressed flowers and leaves
Thin card or thick paper
Notepaper
Book or notepad
PVA glue
A glue brush
A pencil
A ruler
Scissors

Flowery greetings cards

HANDY HINTS

If you don't have enough stems or leaves for the flowers, colour them in with paints or felt-tip pens. You could draw a patterned border around the pressed flowers too.

Pressed flowers are delicate so handle them carefully.

When you are sticking down whole flowers, use a runny glue.

Greetings cards

1. Cut out a long piece of thin card and fold it in half neatly. Decide whether you want your card to stand upright, or longways on its side.

2. Try out different arrangements of flowers and leaves. If your card is going to stand on its side, you could arrange the flowers in a row, as if they are growing.

3. When you have chosen your arrangement, brush glue on the flowers and leaves and down the stems. Press them in place. Cover with the paper and leave to dry.

Bookmark

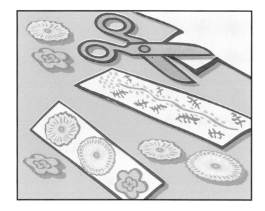

To make a bookmark, cut a strip of card about 15cm long. Glue flowers and leaves on it. Flowers with bendy stems look good, or try single flowers without leaves.

Book cover

Make a book look special by gluing pressed flowers on to the front. Arrange the flowers, leaves and stem to look as if they are still growing naturally.

Folder

Make a pressed flower folder from two pieces of thin card or thick paper. Tape one side of the folder together, and glue on two lengths of ribbon on the other side.

Make and decorate a folder with leaf shapes.

Pressed flowers make a special book cover.

A bookmark

EGG SHELL FLOWERS

When you next eat a soft-boiled or hard-boiled egg, try not to break the shell too much because you can turn it into a delicate flower decoration. It's best to use hard-boiled egg shells but any carefully broken shells will do. If you handle egg shell flowers gently, they will last a long time. Try making lots of them and putting them in a vase or hanging them on a twig.

Things you need

Clean, dry egg shells
Thin sticks and a twig without leaves
Green paper for leaves
Poster paint and paintbrush
Glue
Strong thread
Scissors
A pencil or pen
A pin
A ruler

Hang egg shell flowers on a twig or small branch.

Hanging flowers

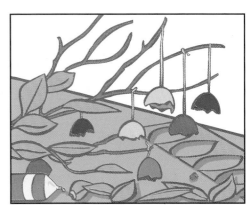

1. Paint the outside of each shell and then the inside. For each shell, cut a length of thread, about 10cm long. Glue one end to the bottom of the shell. Leave it to dry.

2. Dab glue on the points of the twig. Wind the ends of one piece of thread around a glued twig so that the shell hangs downwards. Hang more shells on the twig.

3. Draw leaves on green paper and cut them out. Fold them in half and then unfold them again. Glue the ends and press them on to the branches of the twig.

16

Arrange shell flowers in a vase.

HANDY HINTS

Wash the egg shells carefully, pulling out the thin layer of skin on the inside. Leave them to dry.

Gently break off the top of the shell with your fingers to make a straight edge, or you could make an edge shaped like flower petals.

One way to paint the outside of a shell is to put the fingers of one hand inside it. Then you won't mess up the part you have just painted.

To make lots of paper leaves at the same time, make concertina folds in the paper and then cut out one leaf shape.

Stick flowers

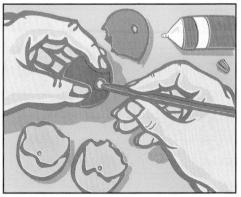

1. Paint the inside of each shell and leave it to dry. Then hold the shell in the palm of your hand and paint the outside. Paint more shells and leave them to dry.

2. Carefully make a small hole in the bottom of the shell with the pin by gently pressing down on the inside. Dab glue on the hole and push the shell on to a stick.

3. Draw leaf shapes on green paper and cut them out. Dab glue on the ends of the leaves. Press them on to the stick and around the base of the flower.

17

COLOURFUL COLLAGES

Here is a clever way of preserving leaves with PVA glue. When this type of glue is wet, it's cloudy, but when it dries, it is clear and shiny.

Collect different kinds of dry leaves, especially ones which are changing colour. You will need a big selection of different-sized, different-coloured and different-shaped leaves to make a really colourful collage.

Things you need

Thin leaves in different sizes, shapes and colours
Small fern leaves
Blades of grass
A pencil
White or coloured cardboard
PVA glue
A brush
Scissors

A woodland picture of a hut with a smoking chimney and a big leaf door

HANDY HINTS

Use the leaves within an hour or two of collecting them, before they start to shrivel and go brown.

When brushing glue over the leaves, stroke the leaves from the stem to the tip.

If the leaves are growing on thick stems, pull them off the stems. Then glue the stems and leaves on separately.

Collage

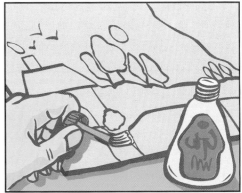

1. Cut out a piece of cardboard to the size you want your picture to be. Lightly draw the outline of the main shapes and think where you will put the different sorts of leaves.

2. Brush a thick layer of PVA glue evenly all over the cardboard, up to the edges. It's best to start by filling in the big shapes and then to fill in the background.

Hang leaf-shaped gift-tags on coloured ribbon.

Make greetings cards with leaves and patterned paper.

3. To make a tree, press down one big leaf or a spray of leaves on to the glue. Use long thin leaves for the trunk. Try making a hut with a chimney from lots of leaves.

4. Use ferns and small leaves to fill in the background. Make a fence from contrasting coloured leaves. Finish off with a border of fat blades of grass.

5. Brush glue all over the leaves, making sure they are completely covered, especially around the edges. Leave the glue to dry and become clear and shiny.

PASTA POWER

Modelling with pasta is great fun. It takes a little patience because you have to wait for the glue to dry before you join the pieces together, but it is well worth the wait! You can make simple or quite complicated models, and the most exciting part is experimenting with your own designs. Try making a pasta car or skyscraper.

Things you need

Various types of dried pasta, such as
  spaghetti, spirals, tubes and shells
PVA glue
Scissors
A brush for the glue
Acrylic or poster paints
A few paintbrushes for the paint
Varnish

A rocket with pasta shell rivets and pasta tube engines

Paint the plane in bold colours and hang it from your ceiling from a strong drawing pin or tack.

A pasta
speed boat

HANDY HINTS

Don't worry if the shape of the model is uneven and has jagged edges and sides. You won't notice this when the model is painted.

When you stick wheels or wings on to your model, you may need to prop it up on corks or bulldog clips. Leave your model to dry in a safe place where it won't be disturbed.

Pasta stunt plane

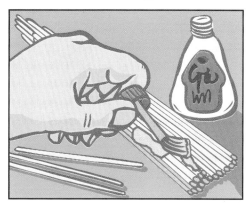

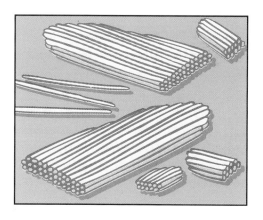

1. Start to make the top half of the body by laying about fifteen pieces of pasta side by side. Hold them together and paint them with glue. Lay another pasta layer on top and paint on more glue.

2. To shape the tail, glue the pasta together in the same way, but as you go, break it into different lengths. When you have built one half of the plane, turn it upside down and build the other half.

3. Make each wing separately. Glue about three layers of pasta together, breaking it into shorter lengths to make the wing tips curve. Make the tailplane in the same way.

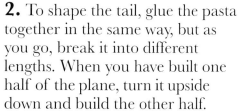

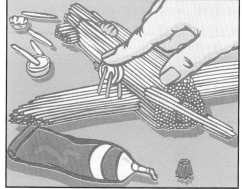

4. Glue the wings to the body, hold them in place and wait for the glue to dry. Then glue on the tailplane. Make a tube of pasta for the nose, and a propeller. Glue them to the front of the plane.

5. Make a curved fin and glue it to the back. Make the front wheels from two pasta spirals and short lengths of spaghetti. Glue them under the plane. Glue one pasta spiral underneath the tail too.

6. Make the cockpit with short lengths of spaghetti. Wait for the glue to dry before you stick it on top of the plane. Paint the plane in bright colours and leave to dry. Paint it with varnish.

AN INDOOR JUNGLE

With the tops of a few vegetables, you can grow your own jungle indoors. When you buy vegetables such as carrots, turnips, parsnips or swedes in the shops, they look dead. But with a little water and time, they will sprout new green tops which can grow quite big. Make an egg head too, which sprouts cress hair.

Things you need for a jungle

Tops of root vegetables, such as carrots, turnips, swedes and parsnips
An old tin tray or a large plate
Kitchen paper
A kitchen knife
A chopping board

Things you need for a cress head

An empty egg shell
Paints and paintbrushes
Varnish
Cress seeds
Kitchen paper

The tops of swedes grow jungly leaves.

Turnip leaves are crinkley and curly.

Jungle

1. Place two layers of kitchen paper on the plate or tray. Make sure the bottom of the plate is covered. Slice about 1 cm off the top of each vegetable with a knife.

2. Put the cut side of the vegetables down on the plate, leaving a small space between each one. Pour water on to the plate until it is about ½ cm deep.

3. Put the plate in a safe place where it is warm and gets plenty of light. Add a little more water every two or three days. Don't let the kitchen paper dry out.

22

Parsnip leaves look delicate.

HANDY HINTS

If you have a fresh pineapple, you can make a 'palm tree' for the middle of your jungle. Keep the top of the pineapple and cut off the leaves. Put it on your jungle tray and it will sprout new leaves that look like the fronds of a palm tree.

If you don't have an old tray or plate for your jungle, use several small polythene food trays pressed close together.

Carrot leaves look like green feathers.

Cress heads

Cress head

1. Wash out an empty egg shell in soapy water and leave it to dry in an old egg box. Paint a funny face on one side of the egg shell. When the egg shell is dry, varnish it.

2. Fold some kitchen paper to make a thick pad. Place it in the bottom of the egg shell. Sprinkle a thin layer of cress seeds on it. Pour a little water on to the seeds.

3. Leave your cress head in a safe warm place. Check every other day that the paper is moist. After a few days, the seeds will start to grow and the egg will sprout hair.

SMELLY THINGS

For centuries people have used sweet-smelling fruit, spices and dried flowers to make their drawers and cupboards smell fragrant. Some people think they also keep the moths away. Make some smelly things to put in your own drawers or cupboards, or to give away as presents.

Things you need for a pomander

A small thin-skinned orange
Whole cloves and a knitting needle
Ground cinnamon
A small plastic bag
A teaspoon
Ribbon

Pomanders smell sweet and spicy.

HANDY HINTS

Pick the flowers for the pot pourri on a warm, sunny morning when they are quite dry.

Collect different kinds of flowers, such as roses, verbena, geraniums, lavender and rosemary.

Pomander

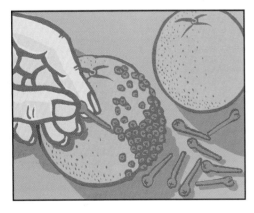  

1. Push the sharp ends of the cloves into the orange. It may help to make holes first with a knitting needle. Push in the cloves close to each other, all over the orange.

2. Put a teaspoonful of cinnamon in the bag. Drop in the orange. Hold the bag closed and shake it to cover the orange with cinnamon. Take out the orange.

3. Tie two pieces of ribbon around the orange, like this. Tie a loop of ribbon on to the knot and hang up the pomander in a wardrobe or cupboard.

Things you need for sweet-smelling bags

Dried lilac flowers or lavender
Thin, pretty fabric
Ribbon
Scissors

Cut a piece of fabric about 20cm square. Put a pile of dried flowers in the middle. Pick up all the corners of the fabric, hold them together and tie a piece of ribbon around the middle. Then tie a neat bow.

Things you need for pot pourri

Rose petals or petals of other sweet-smelling flowers
Ground allspice, nutmeg and cloves
Orris root (which you can buy in a chemist shop)
A screw-top jar and teaspoon
A bowl
A large piece of paper and some small stones

Put your pot pourri in a pretty bowl.

Pot pourri

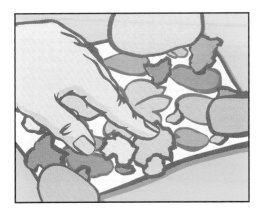

1. Pull the petals off the flower heads. Spread them on to some paper, weighted down with stones. Leave them to dry in a sunny place for a few hours.

2. When the petals are dry, put them in the jar. Add 1 teaspoon each of allspice, nutmeg, and cloves, and 4 teaspoons of orris root. Give the mixture a good stir.

3. Collect more petals in the same way as before, dry them and add them to the jar. Give the jar a good shake. When it is full, pour the petals into the pretty bowl.

25

SEED JEWELLERY

Try making colourful necklaces, bracelets and earrings from clean, dry sunflower, melon or pumpkin seeds. String the seeds together on to strong thread or thin elastic to make jewellery which you can give away as presents or wear yourself. For a special present, you could make a set of matching jewellery.

Things you need

Packets of sunflower and pumpkin seeds (from supermarkets or health food shops)
Necklace, bracelet and earring fixings (from department stores or craft shops)
Poster paint and paintbrushes
Clear nail varnish
A big needle and strong thread
Old newspaper
Glue

Bold blue earrings

Mix the colours and sizes of the seeds to make a pattern.

Paint some seeds green like leaves.

Necklace

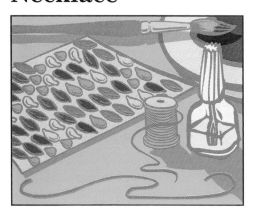

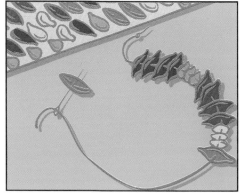

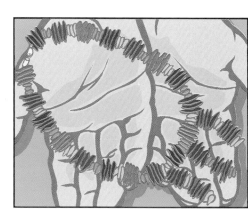

1. Paint the seeds with poster paints on both sides and leave them to dry. Varnish the seeds and let them dry. Cut a 40cm length of thread and thread the needle.

2. Arrange the seeds in a pattern of different sizes and colours. Push the needle through the middle of each seed to string them together. Leave 3cm of thread at each end.

3. Tie fixings on each end. Cut three pieces of thread, about 5cm long. String seeds on to each and knot the ends. Then tie them to the necklace like this.

Flower earrings

1. Paint and varnish enough sunflower seeds to make two flower shapes. Glue four seeds to each earring fixing.

2. Glue on another two layers of seeds. Glue a seed to the centre. Make the other earring in the same way.

Bracelet

3. Cut a piece of thread to go around your wrist. Thread the seeds on to the needle and thread. Tie fixings to the bracelet ends.

A colourful necklace with three seed tassels

HANDY HINTS

When you paint a lot of seeds, put them on clean newspaper, brush one side with poster paint and leave them to dry. Then turn them over and paint the other side.

Experiment with different seed patterns. Tie seeds together in bunches, in lines hanging downwards or lines knotted together.

To help make stringing the seeds together easier, make a hole in the middle of each seed with a pin before threading them on to the needle and thread. It's best to knot each end of the thread twice to make it secure.

27

STANDING STONES

Make your own sculptures of animals, monsters and people from a few clean pebbles and stones. The sculptures can be any size you like but small stones stick together much better than big ones. Paint the sculptures in bright colours. Then give them away as presents or use them as paper-weights.

Things you need

Small clean pebbles and stones
Strong, quick-drying, non-toxic glue
Poster paint
Brushes

A monster animal with a smiley face

A toothy rabbit

A grinning alligator with jagged, zig-zag teeth

A monster animal

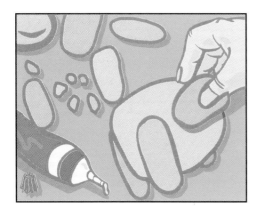  

1. Choose a big flat stone for the body. On one side, stick a long stone for a back leg and a shorter one for a front leg. Wait for the glue to dry before you stick the other two leg-stones in place.

2. To make the head, glue two stones together. Wait for the glue to dry, then stick them on to the head. Glue more stones on top of the body to make humps and bumps, big eyes and a lumpy tail.

3. Before you start to paint your monster, make sure the glue is dry. Paint all over the stones in different colours. Then paint on bright staring eyes, spots and a smiling mouth.

28

Mr Muscle, the strong man

A custard-pie-clown

Bert, the butler

HANDY HINTS

Look for pebbles and stones on the banks of streams and rivers, on the sea shore and in gardens.

Choose stones with flat bottoms, about the size of an egg, which balance on top of each other.

When you stick a stone on to your sculpture, wait for the glue to dry before you stick on another one. While the glue is drying, hold the stones in place with strips of sticky tape. When the glue is dry pull off the tape.

Bert, the butler

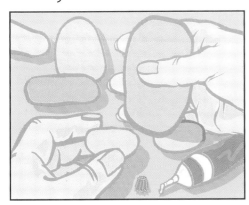

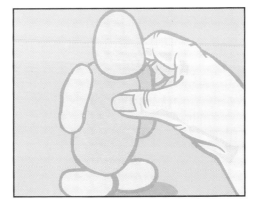

1. Make the body from a big oval pebble. Underneath, glue two pebbles with flat bottoms, which are about the same size as each other. These stones should help to stop the butler wobbling.

2. Glue on a small flat oval pebble for the head. Choose two long flat pebbles for the arms. First glue one pebble to one side of the body. Wait for the glue to dry, then glue on the other pebble.

3. Glue on a tiny pebble for the nose. Paint the head and hands and then add hair, eyes and a moustache. Give the butler a red jacket, and black trousers, shoes and a bow tie.

A MINIATURE GARDEN

Try making your own tiny garden to keep indoors in a warm, light place. It's easy to plant and you can watch things grow. You can plant the garden in a flat terracotta flower pot, but it will grow just as well in an old tray or flat polystyrene food container. Don't forget you will need to water your garden every two or three days.

Things you need

A small tray, polystyrene container
 or flat flowerpot
Small plants or tiny bulbs, and moss
Soil or potting compost
Gravel or small clean pebbles
A small mirror and water

A miniature garden makes a perfect table decoration.

HANDY HINTS

Sometimes you can find moss growing on old walls, on steps or on stones around a pond or lake. Garden centres and florists also sell moss.

You could ask a keen gardener for a cutting or a leaf from a plant. Ask them to tell you how to grow the plant, too. Put the cutting or stem of the leaf in the soil and watch for signs of growth.

Before you water the garden, press your fingers gently on the moss. If it feels damp, don't add any water. More plants die from being over-watered than they do from having too little water.

A mirror 'pond' near a window reflects the blue of the sky and looks as if it's water.

Miniature garden

Choose a mixture of plants with different leaf shapes and flowers.

1. Fill the tray with about 2cm of fine soil or potting compost. Spread it out evenly. Water the soil but don't make it soggy.

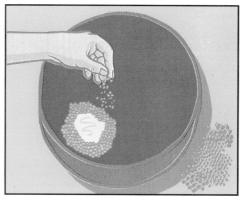

2. Put the mirror on the soil, and press down on it a little. Place small stones around the mirror to hide its edges.

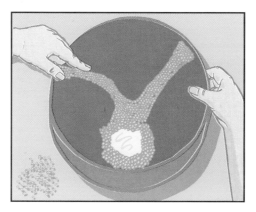

3. Make pathways from small stones. Don't make them too wide because you need plenty of space for the plants in the garden.

4. Make small holes in the soil and carefully push the roots of a plant into each one. Gently press down the soil around the roots.

5. Lay pieces of moss over the soil and around the plants. Place them close together and press down on them firmly.

6. Put the tray where it will get plenty of light. About every two days, check the garden and add a little water if the soil is dry.

BEAN PICTURES

Look for different coloured dried beans, peas, grains and seeds in the kitchen. Ask if you can use them to make all sorts of interesting pictures of people, animals and flowers.

Things you need

Dried kidney beans, borlotti beans, aduki beans, mung beans, lentils, rice, split peas, linseeds, pumpkin seeds, popping corn and couscous
White cardboard
PVA glue
A pencil

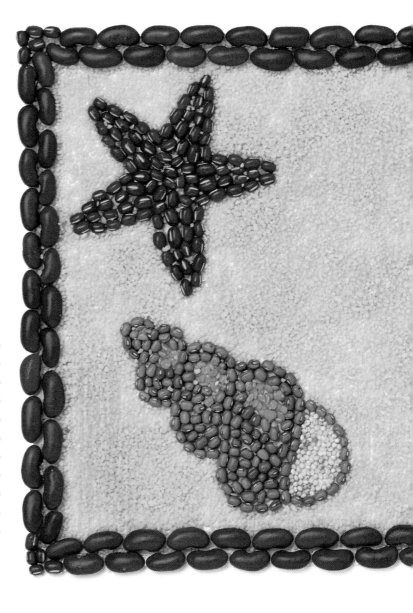

HANDY HINTS

You can buy dried beans and peas in supermarkets and health food shops.

Before you start, shake out of the packets small piles of the beans and seeds that you are going to use. Then the rest won't get messy with glue.

A seaside picture

1. Cut a piece of card to the size you want your picture to be. Draw the outlines of the main shapes. Then think about the sort of beans you will use to fill in the shapes.

2. Brush glue over the scallop shape. Press sunflower seeds along the outside, one by one. To make the shell's ridges, glue rows of seeds in a fan shape.

3. Sprinkle lentils on the scallop shape and press them on the glue. Shake off any which have not stuck to the card. Fill in any gaps by pressing on more lentils.

4. Press fat beans, one by one, on to big shapes, such as the starfish and hull of the boat. Make a mast from linseeds, a flag from green lentils and sails from split peas.

5. To make sea, brush glue over the corner of the picture, sprinkle on the rice and press it down. Shake off any loose grains. Make sand from couscous in the same way.

6. Carefully fill in the crab shape with lentils and small seeds. To make a border, brush glue along the edge of the picture and press on two lines of kidney beans.

SWEET THINGS

Chocolate-coated fruits and frosted fruits are perfect for a party. You can use small, whole fruits, such as grapes or strawberries, or segments of larger fruits, such as tangerines and peeled apples, pears and bananas. The fruits won't last for very long, so it's best to make them on the morning of the day you want to eat them. And remember cooking can be dangerous, especially when you use boiling-hot water, so ask an adult to help you.

Things you need for chocolate fruits

Small fruits or slices of fruit
A bar of milk, white or plain chocolate
A small and a large heat-proof bowl
Toppings, such as hundreds and thousands, chocolate strands and dessicated coconut
A toothpick or cocktail stick for picking up fruit
A spoon
A cake rack
Boiling water

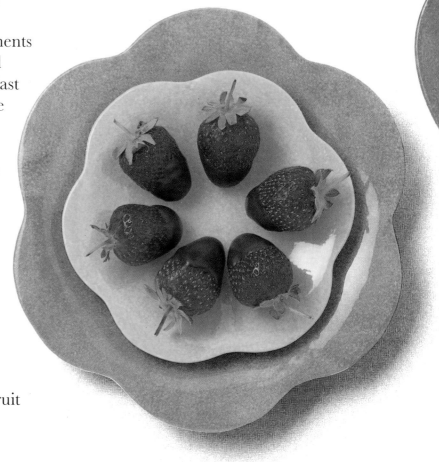

Chocolate-dipped strawberries look even better with their green 'hats' on.

Chocolate fruits

1. Break eight squares of chocolate into the small bowl. Cover it with a saucer. Place it in the big bowl. Ask an adult to pour boiling water half way up the side.

2. Leave the chocolate to melt for about five minutes. Stir it with a spoon. Pick up a strawberry and dip half of it in the chocolate. Then put it on the rack to cool.

3. Pick up another piece of fruit. Dip half of it in the chocolate, then into one of the toppings. Put it on the rack to cool. Dip all of the fruit in this way.

34

Arrange a mixture of
fruits on a pretty plate.

Frosted fruits
sparkle with
sugar.

Things you need for frosted fruits

Small fruits or slices of fruit
A small and medium-sized heat-proof bowl
A toothpick or cocktail stick for picking up fruit
A spoon, cake rack and boiling water
White sugar and jam

HANDY HINTS

Some fruits, such as apples and bananas, go brown after they have been sliced. To stop this happening, toss them in lemon juice before dipping them in chocolate. This won't happen to frosted fruits because the jam will stop any air getting to the fruit and turning it brown.

Frosted fruits

1. Place three spoonfuls of jam in the small bowl and cover it with a saucer. Place it in the big bowl. Ask an adult to pour freshly boiled water half way up the big bowl.

2. When the jam has melted, add two tablespoons of hot water and stir it. Pick up a fruit and roll it in the jam. Try to cover the fruit all over with jam.

3. While the jam is still hot and sticky, roll the fruit in the sugar until it is completely covered. Put the fruit on a drying rack and sprinkle on more sugar.

SAND SCULPTURE

Did you know you can make your own sculptures with decorating filler and sand? When the mixture dries, it is hard and you can paint it with poster paint or you could leave it unpainted to look like a real stone statue. For a rough surface, coat the outside of your finished sculpture with sand. Try making lots of different sculptures of people, animals and monsters.

Make the creases in an elephant's baggy skin with a knife.

Things you need

Clean, dry sand
A packet of decorating filler
A pencil
An old bowl or polythene tub
An old dessert spoon
A stick for mixing
Water
Poster paints and paintbrushes
Old newspapers

A diving
baby penguin

Gus the gorilla

1. Put about three spoonfuls of filler in the bowl. Pour in a few drops of water. Stir the mixture, adding a very little more water until all the powder is mixed in.

2. Add about three spoonfuls of sand to the bowl. Stir the mixture thoroughly. If the mixture is not very thick, spoon in a little more sand and stir it again.

3. Take lumps of the mixture and roll into shapes to make different parts of the gorilla. Make round balls for the head and body, and sausages for the legs and arms.

Paint brown patches on a yellow giraffe. Make the patches smaller on the legs.

HANDY HINTS

Start by making a small sculpture. Then after some practice, try making bigger, more complicated sculptures.

Add the water to the filler only a little at a time so that the mixture is very thick and stiff.

When you have finished making a sculpture, wash your hands quickly before the filler dries. And don't forget to clean up quickly as well because the modelling mixture dries hard.

Gus the gorilla

Give a penguin round, white eyes and an orange beak and feet.

4. Make some slip, which is a watery mixture of filler and water. Bend and fold the arms and legs to fit around the body and stick them to the body with the slip.

5. Paint slip over the top of the body, where the head will go. Press the head in place. You can use a pencil to model the face and feet. Leave the gorilla to dry overnight.

6. Paint the gorilla. You can use the colours of real animals or paint it in fantastic colours. Or you may want to leave the gorilla unpainted to look like stone.

SHELL BOXES

Here's a simple way to decorate small boxes, pots and frames with shells and coloured pebbles. Look for small shells and tiny pebbles when you are on the seashore, on the banks of a lake or a river. Also, you can buy packets of small shells in some craft or novelty shops.

Things you need

Small shells and pebbles
Small boxes, pots and a picture frame
Quick-drying clear glue and PVA glue

Shells make a plain box really special.

HANDY HINTS

Try painting the shells different colours with poster paint. To make the shells shiny, brush them all over with PVA glue.

Use clean small glass jars with lids, or well-washed empty make-up pots. Make sure the pot is completely dry before you start to glue one any shells, otherwise the glue won't stick to the surface.

Shell boxes

1. Before you start, arrange different-sized and different-coloured shells on some paper and experiment making patterns with them. Think carefully about how the shells will fit on the box.

2. To make a shell flower, arrange shells to look as if they are petals on top of the box lid. Glue them to the lid. Glue a small starfish or tiny pebble to the middle of the flower.

3. Choose a mixture of big and small shells to go around the rim of another box. Dab glue on the bottom of one shell and press it on to the lid. Wait for the glue to dry, then stick down the next shell.

Keep jewellery in a pot decorated with shells.

A shell-flower box

Shells and starfish make an unusual picture frame.

Screw-top pot

1. Leave an empty screw-top make-up pot to soak in soapy water overnight. Then wash it thoroughly to make sure all of the label has come off. Dry it on a thick towel.

2. Glue small shells around the rim of the pot and around the bottom. Then glue a different kind of small shell all around the sides and top. Leave the pot to dry in a safe place.

Picture frame

Glue shells around a small mirror or a photograph frame. Arrange the shells in a pattern along the sides, top and bottom. When the glue is dry, brush over the shells with PVA glue to make them shiny.

RICE MASKS

Long ago, at masked balls people would hide their faces behind beautiful masks. Make your own disguise – a mask, decorated with painted rice.

Things you need

Thick white cardboard and PVA glue
Rice (long-grain rice is best)
A thin wooden rod about 24cm long
Poster paints, brushes, a pencil
A small round coin

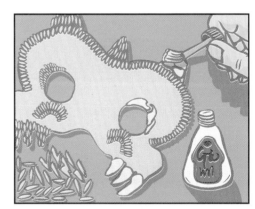

A dramatic
monster face

A monster mask

1. Hold the card up to your face and feel where the eye holes will go. Take the card away and draw round the coin for each eye hole.

2. Draw and cut out a monster mask shape which is wide enough for your face. Carefully cut out the eye holes with a craft knife.

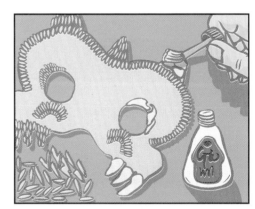

3. Brush glue on the card around the eyes, head, horns, nose and teeth. Carefully stick down the rice close together in neat rows.

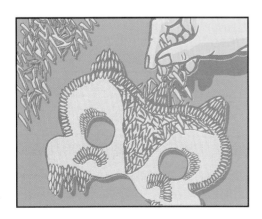

4. Brush glue on the rest of the mask. Sprinkle the rice over the glue, pressing it down carefully to make it stick. Then leave it to dry.

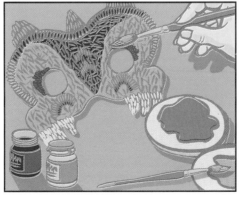

5. Paint each part of the face in bright colours. Allow each different colour to dry before starting to paint on another one.

6. Tape one end of a piece of doweling to the back of the mask. Hold the mask in front of your face and look through the holes.

40

HANDY HINTS

Try using other kinds of rice or small beans to decorate your mask, with grains of a different size and shape.

Paint red and white stripes on the stick of your mask, like the stripes on an old-fashioned barber's pole.

Brush glue over the painted mask and scatter on glitter for a sparkly effect.

Cut out two identical card flower shapes, and glue one on top of the other.

Turn yourself into a sea creature with this octopus mask.

A fun fishy mask

WIND CHIMES

You can make a wind chime with a collection of sea shells. Hang it up where it will catch a breeze and tinkle as the shells gently bump against each other. Try using different kinds of shells but make sure they are all about the same size. Before you begin, make sure your shells are clean and free of things like soil or sand. And only ever collect empty shells, without any animals inside them.

Things you need

10-12 large shells
10-12 small shells
Card
Large roll of sticky tape
A pencil and scissors
A needle and some strong thread
Strong glue

HANDY HINTS

If you hang the wind chime out of doors, put it where it won't get wet in the rain, or the shells may drop off.

The beautiful natural colours and patterns of shells show up better when they are shiny. Add shine to your shells by giving them a coat of varnish.

To add extra colour, paint the shells with poster paint. Try painting each one a different colour, or give them spots and stripes.

Make a wind chime with large shells hanging at the same height.

Hang small shells at different heights.

Shell wind chime

Make a spiral wind chime with large shells.

1. Collect shells which are about the same size. This helps to keep the wind chime balanced and hang properly.

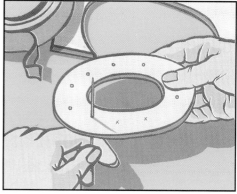

2. Draw round the outside and inside of the roll of sticky tape on to card. Cut out the ring. Make 10 or 12 holes with the needle.

3. Cut 10 or 12 pieces of thread. Each one should be about 40cm long. Carefully tie a knot in the middle of each piece.

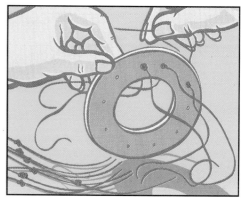

4. Push one length of thread through each of the holes in the ring. Push the ring on to the threads so it rests on the knots.

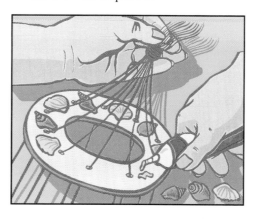

5. Hold the lengths of thread together at the top and tie them in a firm knot. Glue the small shells around the top of the ring.

6. Stick the shells on to the end of each length of thread with strong glue. Wait for the glue to dry, then hang up your wind chime.

FEATHERED FRIENDS

With a few feathers, you can make very realistic pictures of birds that look as if they can really fly. Collect as many clean feathers in different sizes and colours as you can find. Try making the bird pictures into cards or a decorated calendar. You can also make a bird mobile to hang from your ceiling.

Things you need for a flying bird

Feathers
A pine cone
A brazil nut
A long pipe-cleaner
Glue
Paintbrushes
Yellow poster paint
Black poster paint
Thread

Two twirling toucans hanging from the ceiling.

Bend the ends of the pipecleaner to look like claws.

Toucan mobile

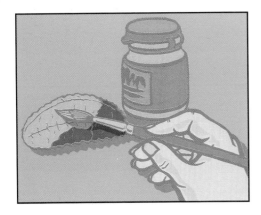

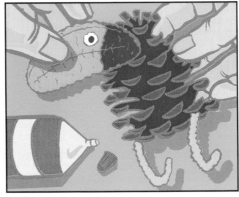

1. Paint a yellow toucan's beak and beady black and white eye on the brazil nut. Paint the rest black. Leave the nut in a safe place while the paint dries.

2. Glue the nut to the top of the pine cone. You may have to break off a few sections before doing this. Bend the pipecleaner around the base of the cone to make two legs.

3. Carefully glue feathers in between the sections all the way around the pine cone. Tie the thread around the top of the cone and hang up the bird.

If you can find only dark or dull-coloured feathers, try painting them. It's best to do this once you have stuck them on the picture.

To help you draw a bird, look at photographs and drawings of real birds in nature books, or make up your own fantastic bird.

You can add more colour to your mobile by painting the tips of the pine cone.

Things you need for a bird picture

Thick white paper or thin cardboard
Feathers and a scrap of felt
A pen or pencil, glue and scissors
Poster paints and paint brushes

Bird picture

1. Lightly draw the outline of a bird on a piece of thick paper or card. You will need to show the head, body, wings, beak, two legs and a short tail.

2. Snip the bottom ends off some feathers. Put a little glue on the back of one feather and press it on to the body. Stick on more feathers in layers.

3. Glue more and more feathers on to the body. Glue on tail and head feathers, too. Make and glue on paper legs and a folded paper beak. Then stick on a felt eye.

STAINED GLASS WINDOWS

With a few different-coloured leaves, you can
make your own stained glass window which will
look magnificent when the Sun shines through it.
You can put it up on your own window or give it
away as a present. You don't need glass but clear
adhesive film with a paper backing. When you
have finished your stained glass window, stick it
on to a window pane with a piece of sticky tape at
each corner.

Things you need

Different-coloured leaves
Clear adhesive film
  (you can buy this in stationery
  and craft shops)
Thin coloured card or thick
  paper for the frame
Scissors
Sticky tape

Stick your stained glass
window to a window
which catches plenty of
sunshine.

Stained glass window

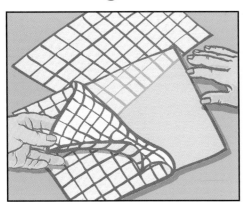

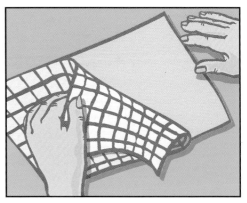

1. Cut two pieces of film the size
you want your window to be. Put
one down flat on a table, film side
down. Take hold of one corner of
the backing and peel it off.

2. Press leaves, one at a time, on
to the film in a pattern. Use
different colours and sizes, leaving
plenty of space between groups of
leaves and around the edges.

3. Lay the second piece of film
down on the table, backing side
up. Take hold of one corner of the
backing and carefully pull it away
from the film.

HANDY HINTS

Often, the paper backing on clear adhesive film has lines printed on it. Cut along these to make straight edges.

Clear adhesive film can be tricky to use. Practise first by making a small window. Then try making a larger one.

If a piece of film without the backing starts to curl up, tape the corners down with small pieces of clear sticky tape.

It's best to use freshly-picked leaves quickly, before they start to curl. Collect the leaves in a very big bag so that they don't get squashed.

4. Hold the second piece of film with the sticky side facing down. Carefully postion it over the first piece of film by lining up the corners and the sides.

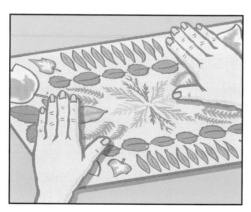

5. Carefully press the two pieces of film together. Smooth out any ridges or bubbles of air. Trim off the edges of film if they don't quite match with scissors.

6. Choose a coloured card for the frame which you think matches the leaves. Cut a window out of the card or thick paper to frame your picture. Tape it at the back.